FUN WITH

Batteries and Magnets

BARBARA TAYLOR

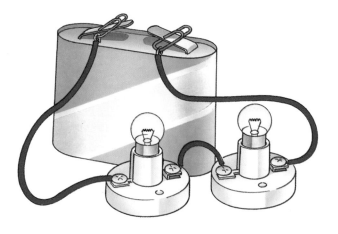

Kingfisher Books

BATTERIES AND MAGNETS

In this book, you can discover how to join batteries, bulbs and wires into simple circuits, more about the pushing and pulling forces around magnets and some of the links between electricity and magnetism.

The book is divided into seven different topics. Look out for the big headings with a circle at each end – like the one at the top of this page. These headings tell you where a new topic starts.

Pages 4–7 Batteries Everyday

Types of battery; how batteries work; using battery power; making batteries; re-chargeable batteries.

Pages 18–21 Switching On and Off

Making switches; two-way switches; dimmer switches; electrical resistance.

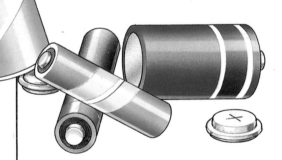

Pages 8–15 Batteries, Bulbs and Wires

How bulbs work; making circuits; series and parallel circuits.

Pages 16–17 Stopping the Flow

Conductors and insulators.

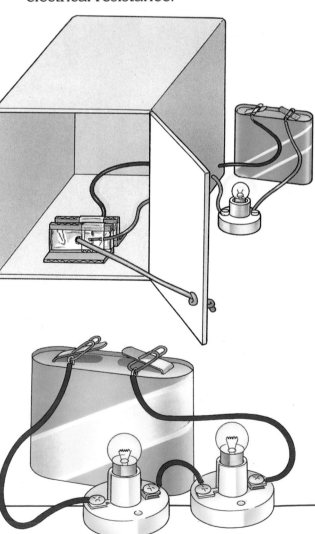

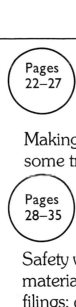

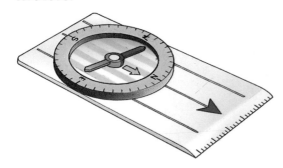

Safety

You should **never** do any experiments with the wires, plugs or sockets in your home or school. The amount of electricity in these things makes them very dangerous. Electric shocks can kill you. Do not go near electricity pylons, overhead cables or sub-stations. Electricity could jump across a gap and kill you.

Look carefully around your home, school and in the shops and see how many different batteries you can find. What shapes and sizes are they? Small batteries are used inside watches, hearing aids and pocket calculators. What other things can you think of that use battery power?

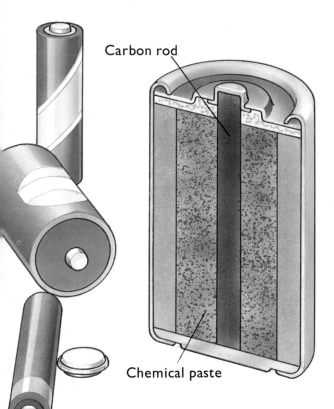

Carbon rod

Chemical paste

Batteries make and store electricity, which is a kind of energy. You cannot see electricity, but you can see that it makes things work. Electricity is made inside a battery by chemicals. Negative electrical charges collect in one part of a battery and positive electrical charges in another. This is shown by the plus and minus signs on a battery. You must **never** take a battery to pieces. The chemicals inside it are dangerous.

Batteries push electricity along wires, and their voltage is the pushing force of the battery. The voltage of batteries, usually printed on the sides, is much less than electricity from a plug or socket on the wall. So batteries are safer to use in investigations. They are also useful because they can be moved from place to place.

▲ How long do the batteries in your toys last before going 'flat'? This happens when chemicals inside a battery are used up. When a battery is worn out, throw it away at once, as chemicals may leak out and cause damage. You should also take batteries out of things you are not going to use for a long time.

 Tongue Tingler

How is a lemon like a battery? This investigation will help you to find out.

Find a short piece of copper wire and a steel paper clip. Poke one end of the wire and the paper clip into the lemon so they are close together but not touching. Touch the free ends of the wire and paper clip on to your tongue. Can you feel a tingle of electricity?

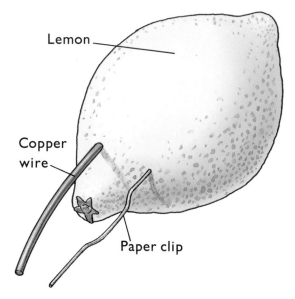

Lemon

Copper wire

Paper clip

What happens

A chemical reaction takes place between the metal wires and the juice inside the lemon. This makes electricity in a similar way to a battery.

 Make a Battery

You will need:
clean shiny coins, blotting paper, salt, aluminium foil, thin wire, a small bulb or a meter that measures electricity.

1. Cut up the foil and blotting paper into lots of small squares. Soak the blotting paper squares in salty water.
2. Make a pile of coins, foil and salty blotting paper, keeping the layers in this order. The bigger the pile, the more powerful the battery.
3. To test your battery, put one wire underneath the pile and touch

▲ This car runs on re-chargeable batteries. They do not go 'flat', but can be re-charged to make the chemical reactions start up again.

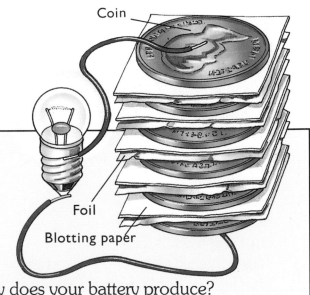

Coin

Foil

Blotting paper

another wire to the top of the pile. If the wires are covered in plastic, the ends must be bare (page 8).
4. Join the wire to a bulb (page 9) or a meter. Can you make the bulb light up? How much electricity does your battery produce?

What happens

Chemical reactions in the pile make electricity, which flows along the wires to the bulb or meter.

BATTERIES, BULBS, WIRES

To find out more about electricity, you can join up batteries, bulbs and wires in lots of different ways. Here are some hints on how to do this.

Wires

Wires are made of metal, which carries electricity, with plastic coating on the outside. The plastic stops the electricity leaking out because it does not carry electricity (pages 16/17). Before you use plastic-covered wire, strip a little plastic off the ends.

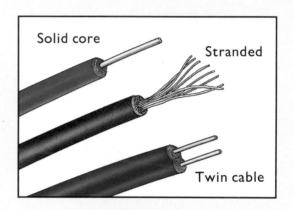

Solid core

Stranded

Twin cable

Batteries

4.5 volt batteries are the most useful for your investigations. It is easier to join wires to batteries with flat ends. The ends of a battery are called terminals. You can use paper clips, crocodile clips or sticky tape to join wires to battery terminals.

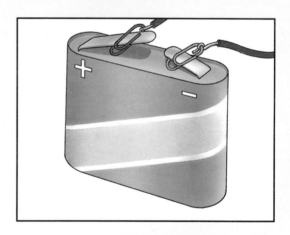

Bulbs

You will need several small, screw-in bulbs – the kind used in torches or bicycle lamps. Use a 2.5 volt or a 3.5 volt bulb with a 4.5 volt battery. Use a 6 volt bulb with a 9 volt battery. You need to touch one wire to the bottom of the bulb and the other wire to the side of the casing.

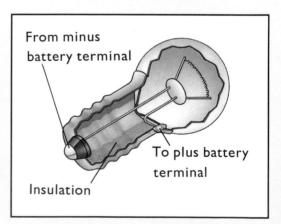

From minus battery terminal

To plus battery terminal

Insulation

► A light bulb is a hollow glass shape full of special gas. The glass is attached to a metal tube with wires inside. Electricity flows into the bulb, up one wire, across a coiled wire called a filament, down the other wire and out of the bulb. The filament is made of very thin wire so it is hard for electricity to squeeze through. The way that wire holds back the electricity is called resistance. This makes the filament so hot that it glows and so gives off light.

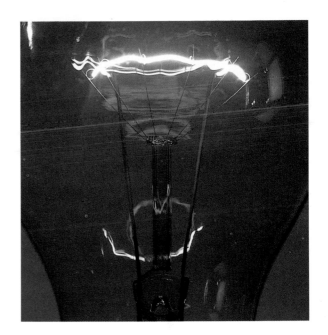

Bulb Holders

When you are doing investigations, it is hard to hold the wires, batteries and bulbs. It helps to fix the bulbs into bulb holders. You can buy these or make some yourself. The pictures show you how to fix the bulb in place.

If you buy one, look at it carefully to see how screws on the side connect up with the two connections on the bulb. To attach the wires to the bulb holder, use a screwdriver to loosen the screws on the sides and fix the wires underneath.

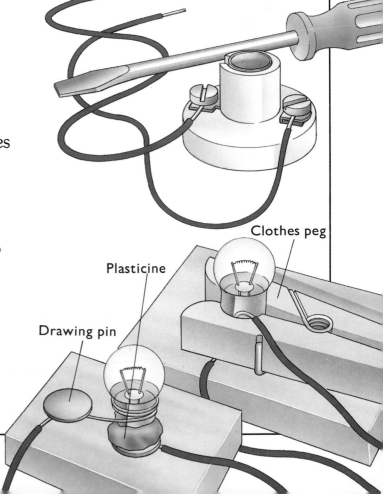

Clothes peg

Plasticine

Drawing pin

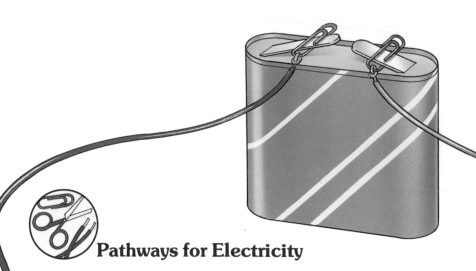

Pathways for Electricity

Can you light up a bulb using a battery and two wires?

1. Fix the bulb firmly in the bulb holder.
2. Clip the end of one wire to the positive battery terminal and fix the other end of the wire to one side of the bulb holder.
3. Join the other wire to the negative battery terminal and the other side of the bulb holder.
4. The bulb should light up. If it does not, check that all the connections are tightly in place.
5. What happens if you use two batteries in series? (Join the negative side of one battery to the positive side of the other).

What happens
Electricity flows from a negative terminal, along the wire, through the bulb and along the other wire to a positive terminal. This pathway along the wire is called a circuit. If the circuit is not properly joined up, electricity cannot flow round the circuit, so the bulb does not light up. When you use two batteries, you have doubled the voltage. Electricity is now pushed around the circuit more strongly, and so the bulb glows more brightly.

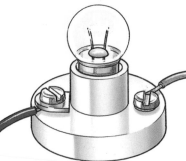

Short Circuits

Do not try to connect one terminal of a battery to the other without putting something like a bulb or a switch (page 18) into the circuit. The electricity will flow very quickly round and round the short circuit, making the wires hot and the battery run down. With re-chargeable batteries, a short circuit can sometimes make the battery itself heat up and melt.

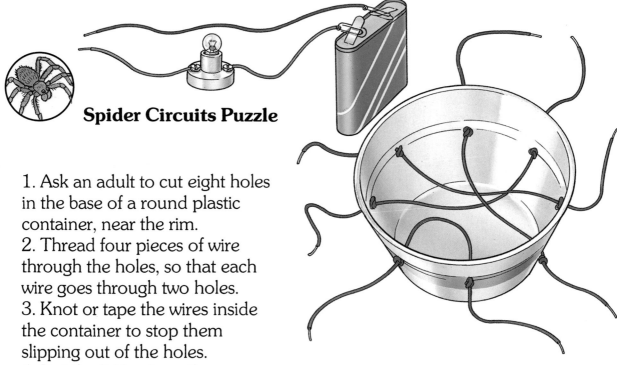

Spider Circuits Puzzle

1. Ask an adult to cut eight holes in the base of a round plastic container, near the rim.
2. Thread four pieces of wire through the holes, so that each wire goes through two holes.
3. Knot or tape the wires inside the container to stop them slipping out of the holes.
4. Put the lid back on the container and decorate it to look like a spider.
5. Give your friends a battery and a bulb in a bulb holder. See if they can work out which pairs of 'legs' go together by making the bulb light up.

What happens
Electricity will only light up a bulb if the circuit is complete. With broken circuits, the bulb will not light.

Make a Quiz Board

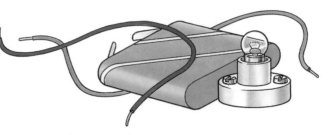

Another way of using circuit tests to solve puzzles is to make a quiz board. Choose any subject you like or know about.

You will need:

a large sheet of thick cardboard, paper fasteners, pens, wire for a simple circuit and wire for the board (or aluminium foil cut into strips), tape or paper, a battery, a bulb in a bulb holder, crocodile clips or paper clips.

Simple circuit

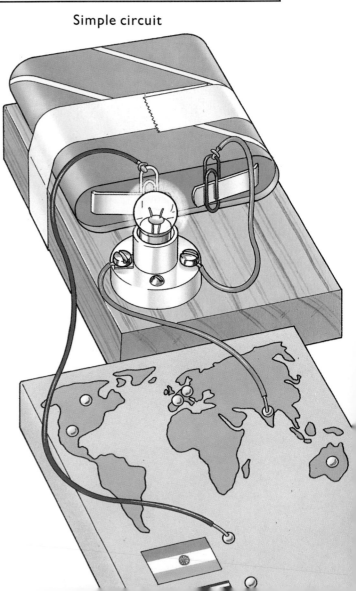

1. Write down or draw some questions and answers on one side of the card. Mix them up, so that questions are not next to the right answers.
2. Push a paper fastener through the board next to each question and each answer.
3. On the other side of the board, use the wire or foil to connect each question with the right answer. Wrap wire or foil round the paper fasteners. If you use foil, put tape or paper between the strips so they do not touch.
4. Make a circuit with the battery, bulb and wires (page 10). Leave the bare ends of the wires free.
5. Touch one wire to a paper fastener next to a question and the other wire to a paper fastener next to the answer you think is

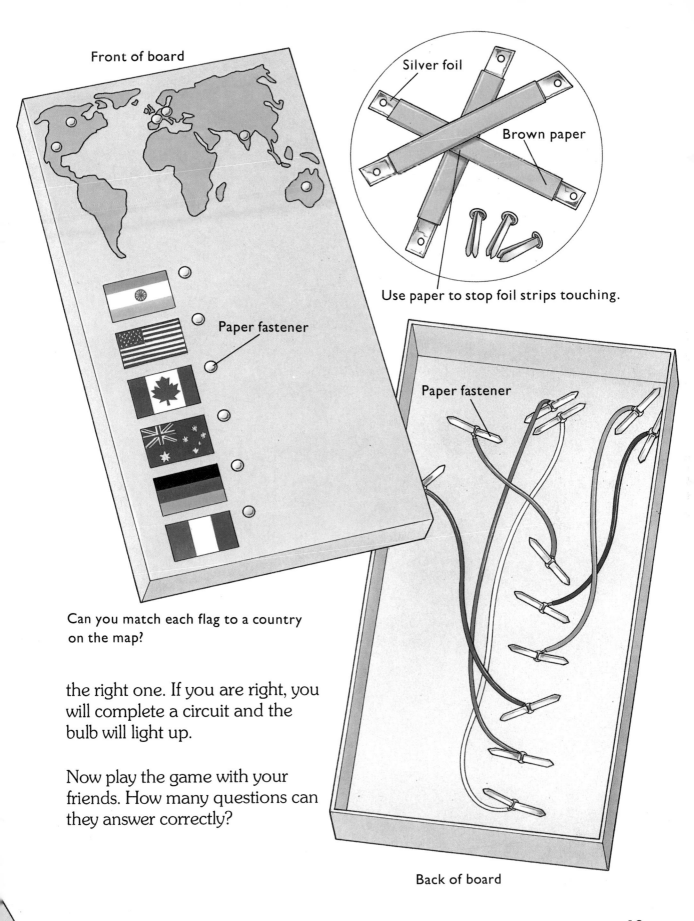

Front of board

Silver foil

Brown paper

Use paper to stop foil strips touching.

Paper fastener

Paper fastener

Can you match each flag to a country on the map?

the right one. If you are right, you will complete a circuit and the bulb will light up.

Now play the game with your friends. How many questions can they answer correctly?

Back of board

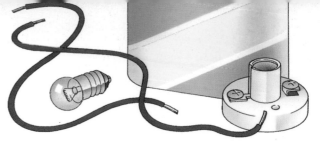

Single or Double Circuits

If you link more than one bulb into the same piece of wire, the same electricity will go through each bulb. So several bulbs will glow more dimly than one bulb on its own. If you take one bulb out, you break the circuit and the other bulbs will go out too. This kind of single circuit is called a series circuit.

There is another way of wiring more than one bulb into a circuit. In a parallel circuit, each bulb has its own circuit. If it has two bulbs, each bulb glows more brightly. If you take one bulb out, the other bulb stays on.

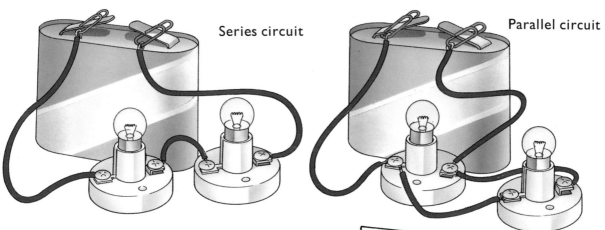

Series circuit

Parallel circuit

See if you can make some series and parallel circuits. You could do some drawings like these to show how the batteries, bulbs and wires are arranged in your circuits.

The wiring in a house is usually arranged on a parallel circuit. If you switch off one light, the other lights stay on.

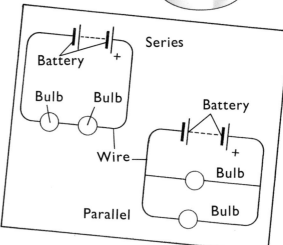

► Christmas tree lights are often wired up on a series circuit. If one bulb stops working the rest of the bulbs go out too. Can you think what else might use a series circuit?

STOPPING THE FLOW

Which materials does electricity flow through? Make a collection of materials to test, such as paper, metal objects (keys, forks and coins), cloth, plastic, a stone, a rubber, cork and wood.

Make a circuit with a battery, a bulb and two wires. Leave the ends of the wires free. Use each object in turn to complete the circuit. Does the bulb light up? Sometimes the paint on objects stops the electricity flowing through. Scratch a little paint off the surface to see if it makes any difference.

▶ The insulators used in power stations or on electricity pylons are made of ceramic materials, such as porcelain. They have an important job to do because the electricity here is at a very high voltage and is extremely dangerous. **Never** go near electricity pylons, sub-stations or power stations. **Electricity can kill you.**

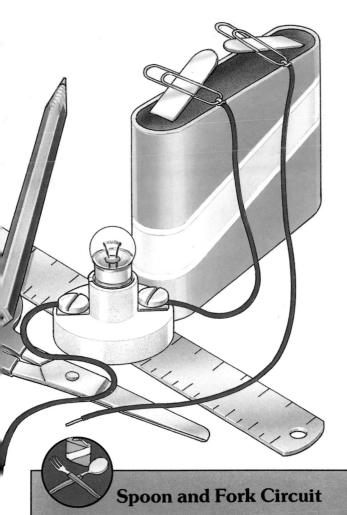

Sort your collection into two groups – materials that let electricity pass through and materials that do not let electricity pass through.

Materials that let electricity pass through them easily are called good conductors. Metals are good conductors, which is why wires are made of metal. Bad conductors are often called insulators. Rubber and plastic are good insulators. Wires are often covered in rubber or plastic. The insulators keep the electricity in the wire and stop it leaking out, so it is less dangerous.

Spoon and Fork Circuit

Can you make a circuit using a spoon and fork to conduct the electricity instead of wires? You will probably need to tape the bulb to the battery to hold it in place.

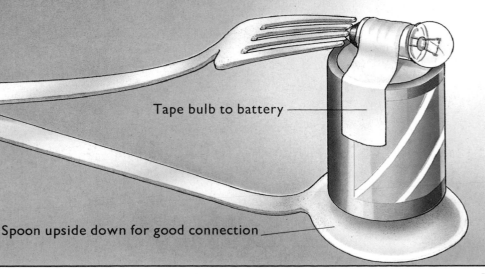

Tape bulb to battery

Spoon upside down for good connection

We use good conductors to make switches. When a switch is off, there is a gap in a circuit so electricity cannot flow. When a switch is on, the gap is closed up to complete the circuit. Electricity can flow right round the circuit to make something work.

Switches are very useful in investigations with batteries, bulbs and wires. Here are some ideas for different ways to make switches:

Paper Clip

Use a paper clip to link two drawing pins. When you move the clip away from one pin, you break the circuit and turn the switch off. You could use card wrapped in foil instead of a paper clip.

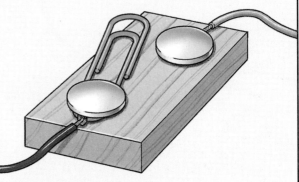

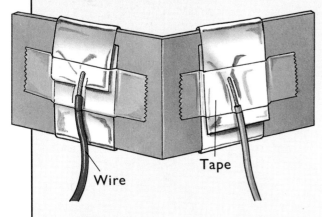

Tape

Wire

Folded Card

Wrap foil around the ends of a piece of folded card. When the folded card presses the two pieces of foil together, it completes the circuit and turns the switch on. This is a kind of pressure switch.

Clothes Peg

Wrap the ends of a clothes peg in foil. A weight pressing on the other end turns the switch off. If the weight is taken away, the foil ends spring together and turn the switch on.

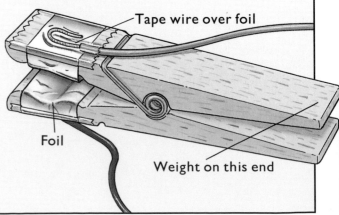

Tape wire over foil

Foil

Weight on this end

 ## Make a Burglar Alarm

You will need:
A large box to make a 'safe', a battery, a bulb or buzzer, cardboard, foil, scissors, sticky tape, string, wire or thread, coloured pencils, treasure for your 'safe'.

1. Cut two pieces of card and wrap them in foil.
2. Fix one wire to each piece of card with tape.
3. Cut two small holes in the side of the box and push the wires through from the inside.
4. Make a circuit outside the box with the battery, the wires and the bulb.
5. Use string or wire to join both pieces of card to the door, as in the picture. Arrange the pieces of card in the 'safe', so that they are not touching.
6. Decorate your 'safe', put some treasure inside and close the door.

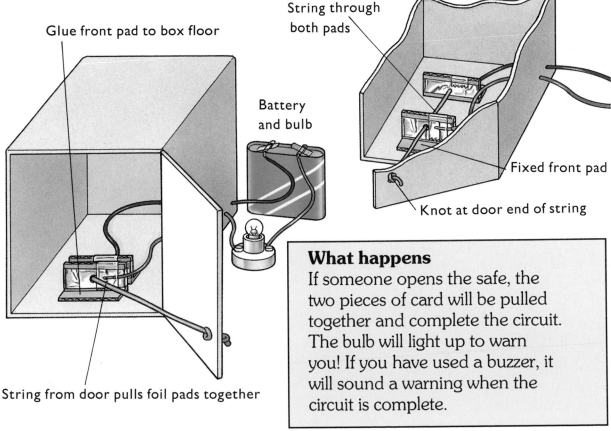

Glue front pad to box floor

String through both pads

Battery and bulb

Fixed front pad

Knot at door end of string

String from door pulls foil pads together

What happens
If someone opens the safe, the two pieces of card will be pulled together and complete the circuit. The bulb will light up to warn you! If you have used a buzzer, it will sound a warning when the circuit is complete.

Make a Two-way Switch

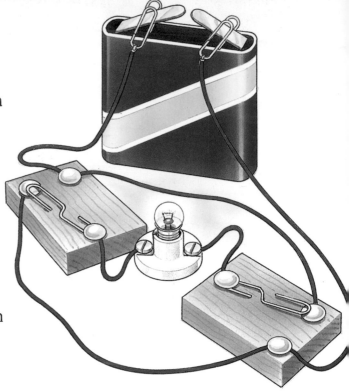

Do you know of a light that can be switched on or off from different places? This needs a special kind of switch called a two-way switch.

You will need to make two switches (page 18) and wire them into a circuit like the one in the picture.

You should find that the bulb can be turned on or off using either one of the switches to break a circuit or complete a circuit. In a building, much longer wires connect the two switches together in a similar way.

Make a Dimmer Switch

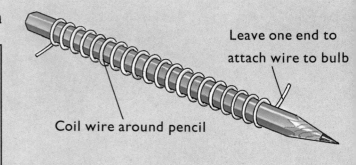

Coil wire around pencil

Leave one end to attach wire to bulb

You will need:
a battery, a bulb, two pieces of plastic-covered wire, a piece of bare wire, a pencil.

1. Coil the bare wire round and round the pencil.
2. Make a circuit with the battery, bulb and plastic-covered wires.
3. Twist the end of one of the plastic-covered wires around the end of the coiled wire.
4. Touch the end of the other plastic-covered wire to the coiled wire at different points. Does the brightness of the bulb change?

▲ Resistors, such as the ones on this circuit board, change the flow of electricity. They are used in light dimmer switches and volume controls.

What happens

When a lot of the bare, coiled wire is in the circuit, the electricity has to push hard through the wire. There is a lot of resistance, so the bulb is dim. If a shorter length of coil is in the circuit, there is less resistance to the electricity. More energy is left to light the bulb, so it glows more brightly.

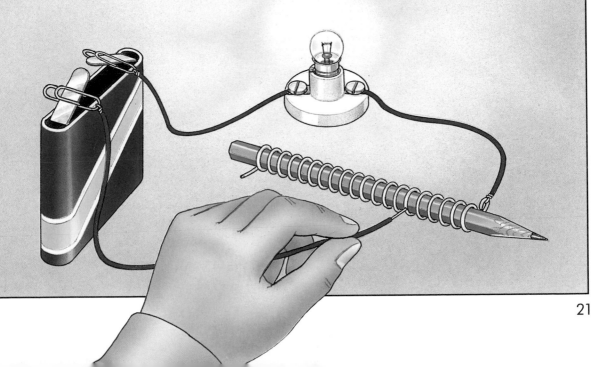

CIRCUITS AND SWITCHES

On the next six pages are some ideas for things to make using circuits and switches. How many more ideas can you think of?

 Make a Lantern

You will need:

a small cardboard box, a bulb holder, a small bulb (2.5 or 3.5 volts), a 4.5 volt battery, a switch (page 18), 2 pieces of wire about 50 cm long, 1 piece of wire about 10 cm long, coloured cellophane, sticky tape, scissors, screwdriver.

1. Cut a large, square hole in three sides of the box. Make a round hole in the fourth side big enough to take two pieces of wire.

2. Glue the cellophane over each of the square holes in the sides of the box.

3. Screw the bulb into the bulb holder and join one piece of the long wire to each side of the bulb holder.

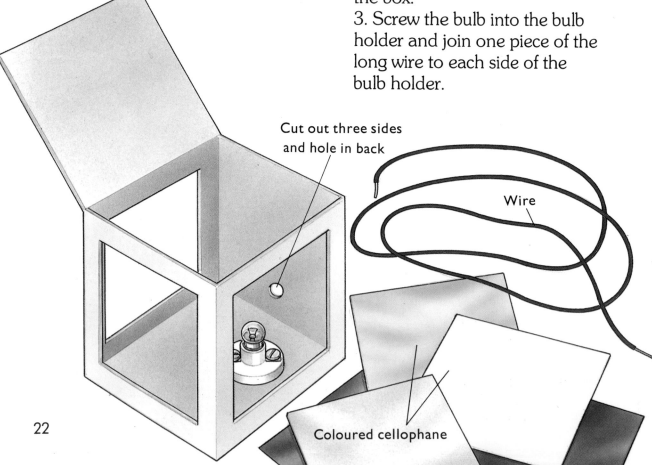

Cut out three sides and hole in back

Wire

Coloured cellophane

22

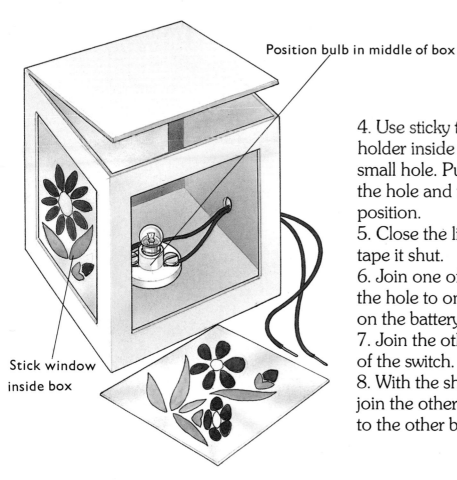

Position bulb in middle of box

Stick window inside box

4. Use sticky tape to fix the bulb holder inside the box, close to the small hole. Pull the wires through the hole and tape them in position.
5. Close the lid of the box and tape it shut.
6. Join one of the wires from the hole to one of the terminals on the battery.
7. Join the other wire to one side of the switch.
8. With the short piece of wire, join the other side of the switch to the other battery terminal.

What happens
When you turn on the switch, you complete the circuit and make the light come on. To make the light flash, you can flick the switch on and off.

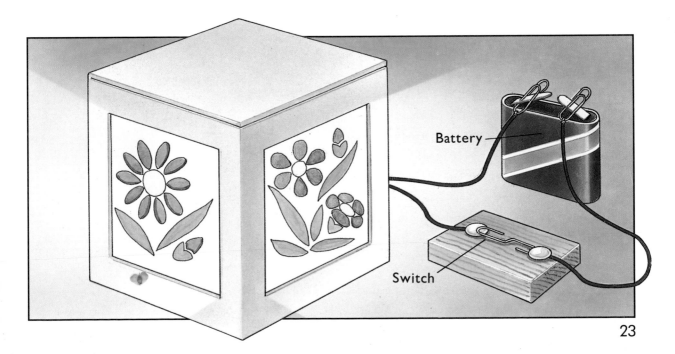

Battery

Switch

Make a Robot

1. Cut away one side of one of the cardboard boxes. Make two small holes with the scissors in the opposite side of the box. This will be the front of the robot's head.

You will need:
4 large cardboard boxes,
4 cardboard tubes, aluminium foil, sticky tape, glue, a 4.5 volt battery, 2 bulbs (3.5 volts), 2 bulb holders, a switch (page 9), 2 long pieces and 2 short pieces of wire, screwdriver, scissors.

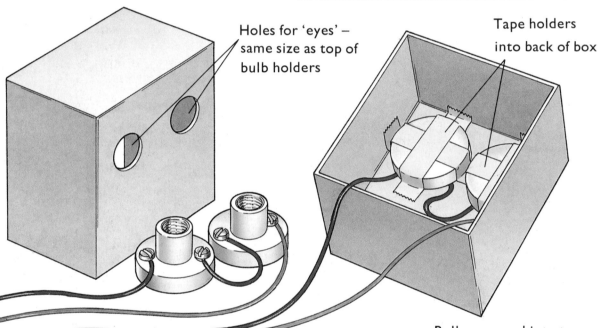

Holes for 'eyes' – same size as top of bulb holders

Tape holders into back of box

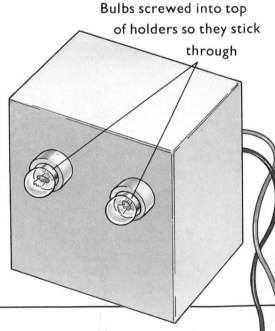

Bulbs screwed into top of holders so they stick through

2. Screw the bulbs into the bulb holders. Join the holders together with a short piece of wire.
3. Fix a long piece of wire to the other side of each bulb holder.
4. Carefully push the bulbs through the holes in the box. Tape or glue them in place inside the box.

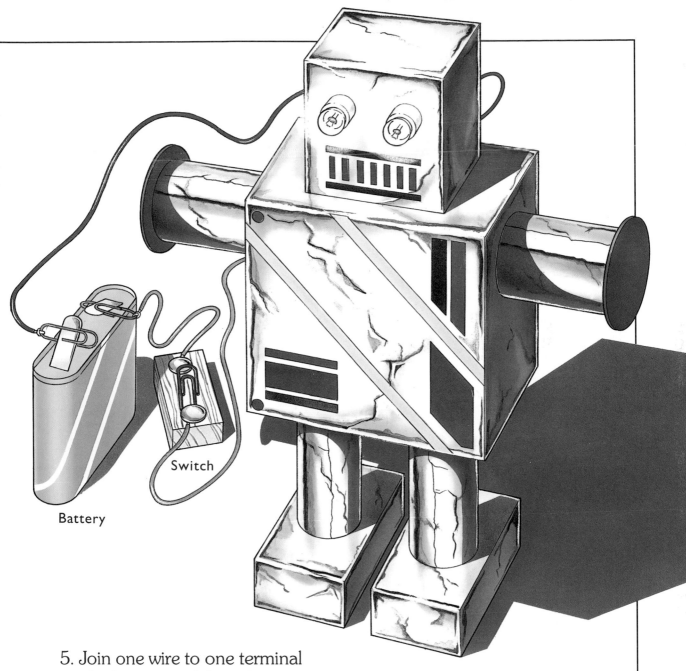

Switch

Battery

5. Join one wire to one terminal
on the battery and the other wire
to one side of the switch.
6. Join the switch to the other battery terminal with the short piece
of wire.
7. Glue or tape the other boxes and tubes to the head to make the
body, arms and legs of the robot.
8. Cover the robot with foil and any other decorations that you like.
9. Flick the switch on and off to complete the circuit and make the
robot's eyes flash.

Make some Traffic Lights

1. Cut two holes towards the top of the thin cardboard. Make the holes one below the other. Cut another hole in the bottom edge of the card directly underneath the two holes.
2. Paint one bulb red and the other bulb green. Screw the bulbs into the bulb holders.
3. Join one long piece of wire to each side of the bulb holders. Push the bulbs through the holes in the card. Tape the back of the holders in place.
4. Join one of the wires from each bulb holder to a battery terminal. Put the battery in the box.
5. Push two paper fasteners through the box lid. Bend back the prongs to keep them in place.
6. Join the free wire from one bulb holder to one paper fastener and the free wire from the other holder to the other paper fastener.

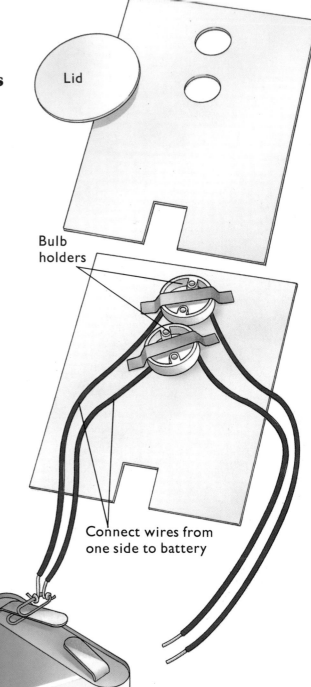

Lid

Bulb holders

Connect wires from one side to battery

You will need:
2 bulb holders, 2 bulbs (3.5 volts), a 4.5 volt battery, 4 long pieces of wire at least 50 cm long, 1 short piece of wire about 10 cm long, 3 paper fasteners, 1 paper clip, a small cardboard box, thin cardboard, red and green poster paints, screwdriver, scissors, tape or glue, paper, paints for decoration, modelling clay.

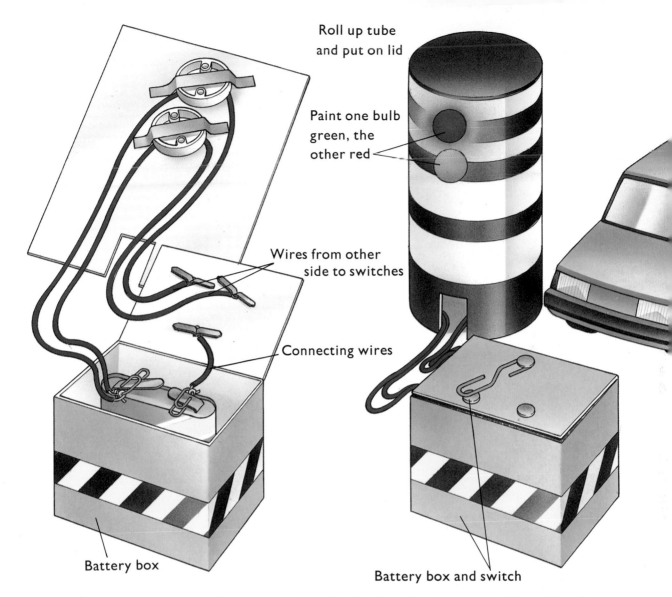

Roll up tube
and put on lid

Paint one bulb
green, the
other red

Wires from other
side to switches

Connecting wires

Battery box

Battery box and switch

7. Push a third paper fastener through the lid of the box and bend back the prongs. Join this paper fastener to the other battery terminal with a short piece of wire. On top of the box, bend a paper clip around this fastener. The paper clip must be able to touch both the other paper fasteners.

8. Close the lid of the box and tape it shut.

9. Roll the thin card into a tube around the bulb holders. Tape the tube sides in place. Pull the wires out through the bottom.

10. Stand the tube upright in modelling clay.

11. Tape a paper circle to the top of the tube, so you cannot see the wiring inside.

12. When the paper clip touches each paper fastener, it completes a circuit and makes the red or green light come on. When you move the paper clip, the lights change.

MAGNETS

Have you got a magnet? What shape is it? Magnets come in all sorts of shapes and sizes, from long, thin ones to the round ones on refrigerator magnets. See how many shapes and sizes you can find.

Magnets are very useful for sticking things together without using glue. They are used to keep the doors of refrigerators shut. They are also used to hold the pieces on the board in travel games. Can you find any other uses for magnets?

Safety with Magnets

Magnets can damage watches, televisions, computer discs, videos and tape recorders. Make sure you keep magnets well away from these things.

▶ The first magnets were made more than 2000 years ago from lodestone, a special black stone which pulls iron materials towards it. It contains an iron ore called magnetite. Nowadays, most magnets are made from iron or steel.

Magnetic Materials

Magnets have the power to pull
some materials, called magnetic
materials, towards them. To see
what is magnetic, collect objects
made from different materials,
such as paper, wood, metal,
plastic, glass and rubber.

Which objects 'stick' to your magnet? Can you feel the pull of the
magnet through your fingers?

Sort your collection into magnetic materials and non-magnetic
materials. To keep a record of your results, you could draw a chart.

Pulling Power

How strong are magnets? Does
the shape or size of a magnet
affect its strength?

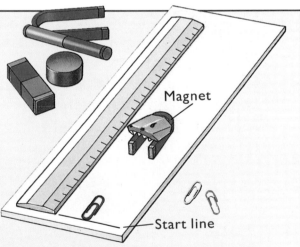

Collect together different
magnets and mark a scale on a
piece of paper. Place a paper clip
at one end of the scale and slide each magnet along the scale from the
other end. Mark where the magnet starts to pull the paper clip towards
itself. Are bigger magnets stronger than smaller ones?

Stopping the Power

Can some materials block the pulling power of a magnet? See if your magnet still works through glass, paper or wood.

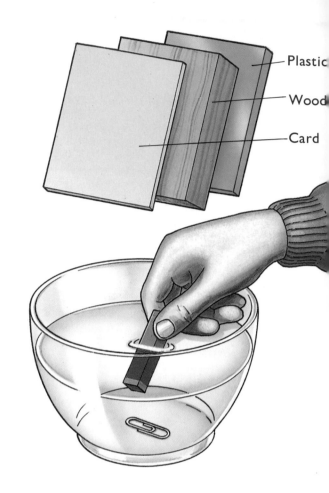

Plastic
Wood
Card

Drop a paper clip into a bowl of water. Can you use a magnet to pick up the paper clip without getting your fingers wet?

Magnetic Maze

1. Draw a maze on one side of a paper plate.
2. Ask a friend to hold the plate for you.
3. Put a paper clip at the start of the maze and hold a bar magnet under the plate.
4. Time how long it takes to pull the paper clip through the maze without touching any of the lines. Have a race with your friend. Who has the steadiest hand?

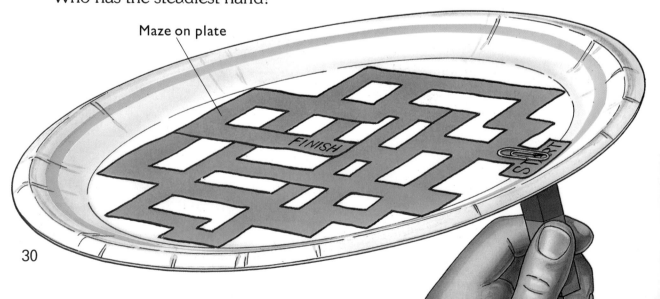

Maze on plate

FINISH

START

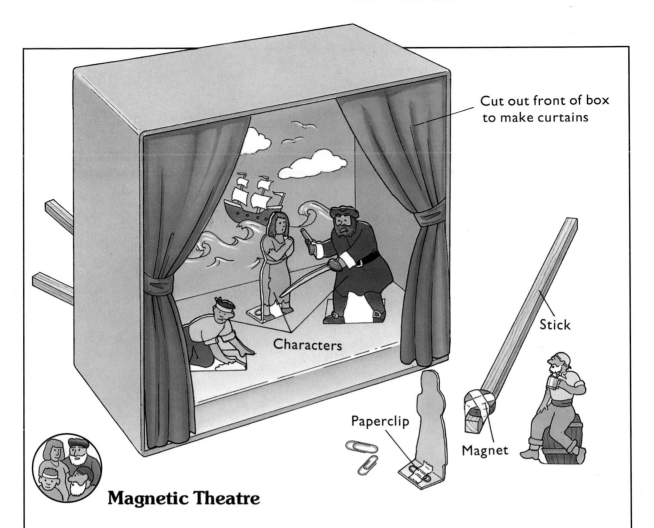

Cut out front of box to make curtains

Stick

Characters

Paperclip

Magnet

Magnetic Theatre

You will need:

thick cardboard, thin card, scissors, paint or crayons, sticky tape, glue, thin sticks, a cardboard box, small magnets.

1. Draw and cut out a model theatre stage from thick cardboard. Colour the scenery and curtains with the paints or crayons.
2. Cut away the top of the box. Turn the box on its side and glue the stage to the bottom and sides. Leave about 4 centimetres space under the stage. Cut away the bottom of the box below the level of the stage. Stick it at the front to hide the gap.
3. Draw and colour in your actors on thin card. Cut them out, with a piece of card at the bottom. Bend this back so they stand up.
4. Tape a paper clip on the bent card behind each actor.
5. Tape a magnet to each of the thin sticks.
6. Put the actors on stage. Slide the magnetic sticks in through the cut bottom of the box, so they are under the stage. Move the actors with the magnets.

 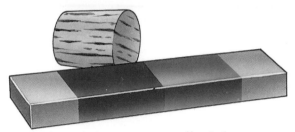

Pull and Push

The pulling force of a magnet is strongest at certain points, called the poles of the magnet. In a long, straight bar magnet, the poles are at either end of the magnet. They are called the North and South Poles (you can find out why on page 34). The poles of one magnet do not always pull the poles of other magnets towards them. Sometimes they push them away. This investigation will show you more about how magnets behave.

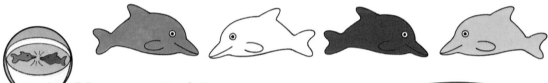

Magnetic Dolphins

1. Draw two dolphin shapes on cardboard. Cut them out.
2. Glue or tape bar magnets to two corks and stick a dolphin on top of each cork and magnet.
3. Float the dolphins in a bowl of water. What happens when you push the dolphins together?
4. Turn one of the dolphins around. What happens?

What happens
The dolphins stick together if the magnets are one way round. But when you turn one magnet around, it will push the other dolphin away. Two North Poles or two South Poles will push each other apart, but a North Pole and a South Pole will stick together. Magnets will stick together if the poles are different, and will push each other apart if the poles are the same.

Magnetic Patterns

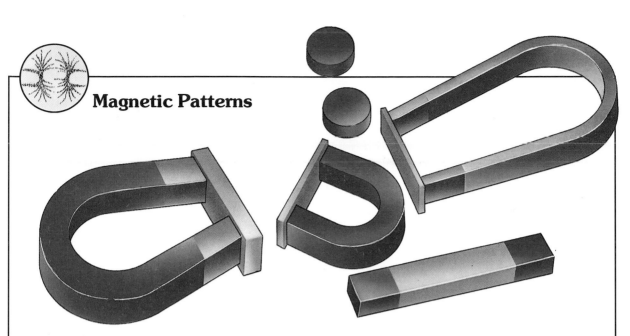

Round magnet: poles around edge

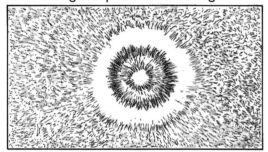

Horseshoe magnet: poles at end

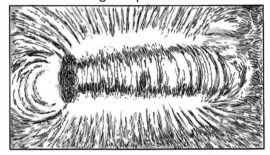

Bar magnet: different poles (at ends) pull together

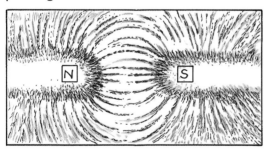

Bar magnet: same poles (at ends) push apart

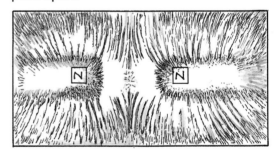

We cannot usually see the pushing and pulling forces around a magnet. But by scattering some iron filings on a piece of paper and placing a magnet under the paper, some of the lines of force become clear. Where the magnet gives out a strong force, lots of iron filings group together. Where the force is weaker, the filings are further apart.

With two poles that are the same, the filings show that the poles are pushing apart. With two poles that are different, the filings show how the poles pull together.

 Pointing North and South

If you hang a magnet up by a thread or float it on water, it spins slowly. When it comes to rest, it points towards the North and South Poles of the Earth. (This is why magnets are said to have North and South Poles.) The Earth itself has magnetic powers and is like a giant magnet. The Earth's huge magnetic force pushes and pulls smaller magnets. Did you know that a compass needle is a magnet?

To find out more about magnets, make one yourself.

Make a Compass

You will need:
a magnet, a needle, a piece of cork or polystyrene, a bowl of water, a compass.

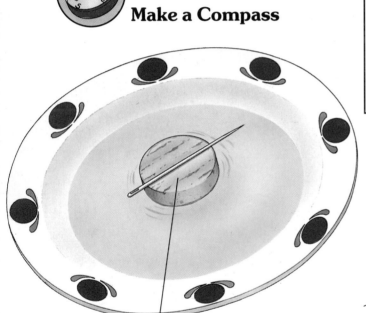

Cork with needle on top

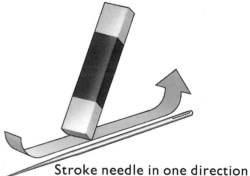

Stroke needle in one direction

1. Stroke the end of the magnet along the needle about 50 times. Stroke it in the same direction each time and hold the needle away after each stroke. This will turn the needle into a magnet.
2. Put the needle on top of the cork or polystyrene and float it in the bowl of water.
3. Place a compass next to the bowl of water and check that your needle points in the same direction as the compass needle.

34

▲ Lodestone (meaning 'the stone that leads') was used to guide people centuries ago. Nowadays, magnetic compass needles are used on ships and aeroplanes as well as on land to help people find their way.

Did you know that you can make magnets with electricity? When electricity flows along a wire, it makes the wire magnetic. You can test this by building a circuit with a switch. Put a compass near the wire and watch to see what happens to the compass needle when you switch on the electricity.

What happens
The magnetic force in the wire will push and pull the magnetic compass needle and make it swing about.

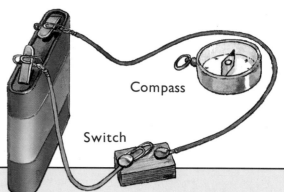

Compass

Switch

Make an Electro-magnet

Iron bolt

If a wire carrying electricity is wound into a coil, it produces a stronger magnetic force than a straight wire. And if an iron bar is placed inside the coil of wire, the magnetic force is stronger still. Make an electro-magnet to see how this works.

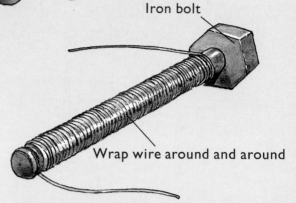

Wrap wire around and around

1. Wind the long piece of wire round the bolt, keeping the coils close together. The more times you wind the wire round the bolt, the stronger the magnet.
2. Join one end of the wire to a battery terminal and the other end of the wire to the switch.

You will need:
a large iron bolt, a nail, 2 metres of wire, a short piece of wire, a switch, a battery, paper clips, a matchbox, a wooden frame, thread.

▲ This electro-magnet is sorting scrap metals from other non-magnetic materials. Electro-magnets are useful because they only work when electricity is switched on.

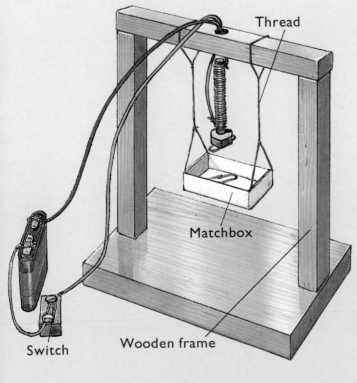

Thread

Matchbox

Switch

Wooden frame

3. Use the short piece of wire to join the other side of the switch to the battery terminal.

4. When the electricity is on, how many paper clips can the bolt pick up? How far away can it attract a clip hanging from some thread?

5. Hang a matchbox from a wooden frame, with your bolt hanging above it. Turn on the electricity, so a paper clip sticks to the bolt. Swing the matchbox and turn off the electricity. Can you catch the clip in the box?

▲ In a bicycle dynamo, a magnet moves when the wheel turns and produces electricity. This makes the bicycle lamp come on. When the cyclist stops pedalling, the magnet stops moving. No electricity is produced, so the lamp goes out. Dynamos use magnets and movement to make electricity.

Making Things Move

An electric motor works in the opposite way to a dynamo. It uses magnetism and electricity to produce movement. Make a motor yourself to see how they work.

1. Ask an adult to push a knitting needle through two corks, one large and one small.
2. Wind some copper wire about ten times round the large cork. Tape the ends to the smaller cork.

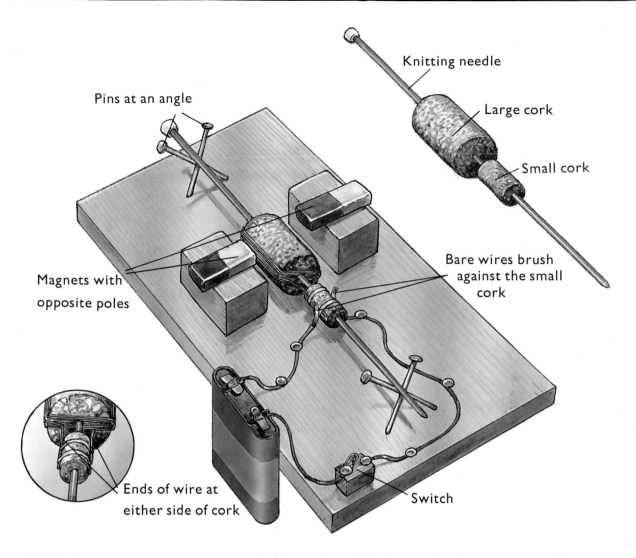

Knitting needle

Large cork

Small cork

Pins at an angle

Bare wires brush against the small cork

Magnets with opposite poles

Ends of wire at either side of cork

Switch

3. Push some pins into a wooden board and balance the knitting needle on the pins. Make sure the corks can turn freely as the needle turns.
4. Balance two bar magnets on top of wooden blocks either side of the cork.
5. Make a circuit with a battery, some short wires and a switch. Fix the short wires to the board with drawing pins.
6. Touch the bare ends of the battery wires to the wires taped on the small cork. When you turn on the switch, the corks should turn round.

What happens
When electricity passes through the coils of wire around the large cork and back to the battery again, it makes the wire magnetic. When this magnetic force meets the magnetic force between the two magnets, it makes the cork turn round.

INDEX

Page numbers in *italics* refer to illustrations or where illustrations and text occur on the same page.

Adviser: Robert Pressling
Designer: Ben White
Editor: Catherine Bradley
Picture Research: Elaine Willis

The publishers wish to thank the following artists for contributing to this book:
Peter Bull; page headings, pp.8/9, 14, 26/27, 32/33, 34; Peter Dennis of Linda Rogers Associates pp.36/37, 38/39; Kuo Kang Chen: cover, pp.4/5, 16/17, 20/21, 22/23; John Scorey: pp.6/7, 10/11, 12/13, 18/19, 24/25, 28/29, 30/31.

The publishers wish to thank the following for kindly supplying photographs for this book:
Page 5 ZEFA; 7 Science Photo Library; 9 Ron Boardman; 15 ZEFA; 16 National Grid Company; 21 Science Photo Library; 28 IMITOR; 35 Chris Howes; 37 Science Photo Library; 38 ZEFA.

Kingfisher Books, Grisewood and Dempsey Ltd
Elsley House, 24–30 Great Titchfield Street, London W1P 7AD

First published in 1991 by Kingfisher Books

© Grisewood and Dempsey Ltd 1991

British Library Cataloguing in Publication Data
Taylor, Barbara
  Batteries and Magnets
  1. Electricity. Magnetism.
  I. Title II. Series
  537

ISBN 0 86272 748 0

Phototypeset by Southern Positives and Negatives (SPAN), Lingfield, Surrey
Colour separations by Scantrans pte Ltd, Singapore
Printed in Hong Kong